THe 5-minute MinDfulness Journal for Teens

PRACTICES TO IMPROVE FOCUS, RELIEVE ANXIETY, AND FIND CALM

Kristina Dingus Keuhlen, PhD, LMFT

ROCKRIDGE
PRESS

Interior and Cover Designer: Chiaka John
Art Producer: Sara Feinstein
Editor: Eliza Kirby
Production Editor: Ruth Sakata Corley
Production Manager: Riley Hoffman

Illustration used under license from Shutterstock and iStock.
Author photo courtesy of Jazzella McKeel

Paperback ISBN: 978-1-63878-381-7
R0

THIS BOOK BELONGS TO:

_____

Welcome to Mindfulness

Hello and welcome! I am so glad you're here. I am Dr. Kristina Dingus Keuhlen, and I began my mindfulness practice to manage my own anxiety struggles about 10 years ago. Some days I hit all my goals, and some days I don't. When this happens to you, just begin again, and again, and again. It's called a practice for a reason! There is no finish line, no gold medal, and no award for being "the best mindful person." As a licensed marriage and family therapist, I have been teaching clients to incorporate mindful practices in their daily lives since 2015.

Teens face an extraordinary amount of pressure and are constantly bombarded with information and influence from friends and social media. It can be difficult to tune out all the noise and just be your authentic self. Mindfulness can help.

Mindfulness is intentional, focused awareness of what you are doing, what you notice with your five senses, and being fully in that moment. You learn to leave past worries behind and minimize concerns about the future by allowing yourself to enjoy what is in front of you, in the present.

Journaling helps slow down our brain's multitasking process that can keep us from being present. It can also help us identify the positive, create moments of calm and clarity, and increase optimism, hope, and gratitude. The best part? You can have a mindful journaling practice in just a few minutes a day—small steps lead to big results!

HOW to USE THiS JOURNAL

This journal is divided into four parts: body, thoughts, emotions, and changing behaviors. There is no right or wrong way to use this journal, but it is recommended to go through the journal in order. The good thing is that no matter how you approach this process, you cannot fail. As I said, mindfulness is a lifelong practice, so find what resonates with you.

In this journal, you'll use mindfulness to become more in tune with your thoughts, feelings, and emotions in a way that is authentic to you. As you complete the prompts and practices, you'll learn self-awareness and get better at being present. The prompts are spaces for you to write openly, without fear of judgment. They will challenge you to go deep within yourself and be emotionally vulnerable. The practice pages will guide you in mindful activities to minimize stress while maximizing relaxation.

Some of the topics are deep, so if you need to take a break or come back to something later, that is completely fine. It is also okay to ask a trusted adult or friend for support if you have trouble with a prompt. If you need additional support, there's a list of mental health resources at the end of the book.

I encourage you to find a set time to dedicate five minutes a day to this journal. Just like a muscle, it will always be there to support you, but the more you use it, the stronger it grows. The more you practice living mindfully, the more natural it will become.

PART ONE

Pay Attention to Your Body

In this section, you will learn to notice physical sensations throughout your body. People often attempt to push aside or ignore unpleasant emotions or sensations, such as sweaty palms or increased heart rate. But these can actually be cues for you to slow down and take a few deep breaths.

Being in tune with your body can help provide important information about what you need. Here you will learn to identify and understand these needs. Sometimes the need is as simple as taking a deep breath, drinking water, or feeling the sunshine on your skin.

While you're responding to the prompts in this section, start to pay attention to what is going on in your body as you are answering the questions.

What do you notice about how your body feels right now? Relaxation? Stiffness? Tension? Neutrality?

_____

_____

_____

When do you pay attention to your body? When it is strained or in pain? When do you feel strong or relaxed?

_____

_____

_____

On a typical day, what do you tend to notice about your body? (*Nothing* is a perfectly acceptable response.)

_____

_____

_____

What time of day does your body typically feel its best? What does this feel like to you?

_____

_____

_____

What is your favorite part of your body and why? Do you like the way it feels? Do you like the way it looks?

_____

_____

_____

Which part of your body could you learn to like more? Why do you think you struggle to like this part of you?

_____

_____

_____

Write a note of appreciation to your favorite part:

_____

_____

_____

Write a note of appreciation to the part you are learning to love:

_____

_____

_____

Describe your hair. Is it short or long? Coarse or thin? Straight or wavy?

_____

_____

_____

Look at your eyes. Do you notice any color variations between them? Are they symmetrical or are there differences?

_____

_____

_____

What do you notice about your skin? Is it the same all over your body, or do you notice areas where it may have different textures?

_____

_____

_____

When you observe your body in this way, what comes up for you emotionally?

_____

_____

_____

What makes you feel strongest in your body?

_____

_____

_____

When your body feels strong, how do you feel emotionally?

_____

_____

_____

On days when you feel less strong, how does that impact your mood?

_____

_____

_____

How do you move your body every day? Does this movement encourage you to feel mentally and physically fit?

_____

_____

_____

_____

What do you notice physically and emotionally when you get "hangry"?

_____

_____

_____

Describe your favorite go-to snacks. What do you love about this food?

_____

_____

_____

If you could only eat one thing for the rest of your life, what would it be and why? How does your body respond to you thinking about this one thing?

_____

_____

_____

Write a note of gratitude for your favorite meal:

_____

_____

_____

_____

Mindful eating is a process that helps us slow down, engage our senses, and increase our body appreciation. All bodies are beautiful and deserving of love and nourishment. We do not have to "earn" the right to eat!

Choose a small snack that can easily be held in your hands, doesn't require cutlery, and doesn't make a mess.

1. Hold the food in your hand and observe.

2. Notice how it feels. Is it smooth or textured? Is it one piece or many?

3. Take a deep breath in and smell. Is it consistent or does the smell change?

4. When you place the item in your mouth (don't chew yet), does your mouth agree with what your eyes and nose observed?

5. Taking another deep breath, slowly chew at least 10 times before swallowing.

What do you notice after this practice?
How do you feel physically and/or emotionally?

_____

_____

_____

_____

_____

We can often be our harshest critic, especially when it comes to talking to ourselves about our bodies. Think of a time when you were hard on yourself. What happened? What did you say to yourself?

_____

_____

_____

How does your body feel when you're upset at yourself?

_____

_____

_____

As you are thinking of these difficult questions, what do you notice in your body now?

_____

_____

_____

What might you say to a friend for encouragement that you could say to yourself?

_____

_____

_____

What situations contribute to your feelings of stress and overwhelm? Test anxiety? Friend drama? Your sibling "borrowing" something without permission?

_____

_____

_____

How do you typically react when you get into this mode? Are these strategies helpful or harmful?

_____

_____

_____

Where did you learn these strategies?

_____

_____

_____

What is one thing you can do differently the next time you are feeling anxious?

_____

_____

_____

When you feel overwhelmed, stressed, or anxious, what symptoms usually pop up in your body? Sweaty palms? Racing heart? Upset stomach?

_____

_____

_____

What behaviors do you exhibit when you are in this state that others may notice? Irritability? Snappiness? Short responses?

_____

_____

_____

Do you tend to notice your emotions or the physical sensations first when you are feeling this way?

_____

_____

_____

What is one exercise you could implement to help minimize the physical sensations?

_____

_____

_____

Describe a time when something was so awesome or amazing it took your breath away:

_____

_____

_____

Thinking back to this time, describe how you felt physically or emotionally:

_____

_____

_____

What was so special and/or magical that made your breath catch? Was anyone with you? Did they add to the experience?

_____

_____

_____

If you could re-create this time, what, if anything, would you change? Or was it perfect the way you remember?

_____

_____

_____

Laughter is a great way to observe the mind-body connection and decrease stress. How does it feel to laugh?

_____

_____

_____

When was the last time you laughed so hard your face hurt, your eyes teared up, or you snorted? Who was with you? What was so funny?

_____

_____

_____

Who has your favorite laugh? What do you love about it?

_____

_____

_____

Who is the "funny" one in your family? What do they do to get a laugh?

_____

_____

_____

When you laugh, even for a few moments, you decrease your levels of the stress hormone cortisol and increase your levels of feel-good chemicals called beta-endorphins—pretty cool, right? Try it now.

1. Do a quick body scan from head to toe and see if you notice any tightness or tension. Take a deep breath in and notice any physical shifts or changes.

2. Think of something that made you laugh or smile recently.

3. Imitate your favorite person's laugh. Next, try a loud, silly laugh, or force yourself to laugh until your natural laugh kicks in.

4. Take another deep breath in and do another quick scan of your body to see if tense or tight areas feel more relaxed.

What do you notice after this practice?
How do you feel physically and/or emotionally?

_____

_____

_____

_____

_____

_____

_____

What type of music do you tend to listen to and why?

_____

_____

_____

When you are listening to this music, what feelings do you notice? Does it help you relax, get you excited, change your vibe?

_____

_____

_____

How do you incorporate music into your life? Is it a must-have or can you live without it?

_____

_____

_____

If you had to explain your favorite band to someone, how would you describe them?

_____

_____

_____

How do you feel about background noise?

_____

_____

_____

If you had to choose between white noise or no noise, which would you choose and why?

_____

_____

_____

Do you prefer to be in a loud or quiet environment? If it depends, share what situations you like for each type:

_____

_____

_____

Would you consider yourself to be a loud or a quiet person? Is this similar to or different from the rest of your family members?

_____

_____

_____

What do you enjoy about weekends? More free time? Catching up on sleep? Are you super busy with sports, friends and family, and hobbies?

_____

_____

_____

_____

If you could do anything that you used to love doing on the weekends when you were younger, what would it be? What's holding you back from doing that now?

_____

_____

_____

_____

What are some differences in what you enjoy doing now versus what you used to do when you were a kid?

_____

_____

_____

_____

_____

Are you more of an indoor person or an outdoor person?
Why do you think that is?

_____

_____

_____

What do you prefer about your favorite place? Is it the natural
beauty of the outdoors or the peacefulness of being safe and
cozy inside?

_____

_____

_____

What do you think your life would be like if you enjoyed the
opposite of your current favorite place?

_____

_____

_____

What, if anything, is holding you back from exploring the
alternate option?

_____

_____

_____

What do you love about your favorite song? When was the last time you heard it?

_____

_____

_____

When you think of your favorite candy, what comes to mind? When was the last time you enjoyed it?

_____

_____

_____

Who is your favorite person or favorite pet? What about them do you love?

_____

_____

_____

As you think about some of your favorite things, what do you notice in your body? Any physical shifts?

_____

_____

_____

_____

Progressive muscle relaxation helps you engage each part of your body while you pay attention to your breathing and notice the shifts you experience.

1. Get into a comfortable position where you feel safe, preferably lying down.

2. Flex and release each part of your body, starting from your toes up to your face.

3. When you flex a muscle group, inhale for a count of four. When you release the muscles, exhale for a count of four. In this way, your breathing matches the tension and release of each muscle group.

4. Move through your feet, calves, knees, thighs, glutes, hips, stomach, pecs, fingers, hands, forearms, shoulders, jaw, ears, and eyebrows.

5. Take a few additional breaths when you are done, and slowly come back to a seated position.

What do you notice after this practice?
How do you feel physically and/or emotionally?

_____

_____

_____

_____

_____

_____

In what situations do you feel absolutely comfortable listening to your gut instincts (also known as your intuition)?

_____

_____

_____

Describe a time when you didn't listen to your gut instincts. What happened?

_____

_____

_____

When do you struggle the most with following your intuition?

_____

_____

_____

What is one thing you can do to better learn to trust your instincts?

_____

_____

_____

What is your relationship with rhythm, dancing, and movement?

_____

_____

_____

How do movement and dancing feel for you when you're in the moment? If you are not into these things, describe how you think it feels for someone who is:

_____

_____

_____

Describe how movement and dancing engage the five senses:

_____

_____

_____

When you think of dancing, what comes to mind? Any particular person or specific place?

_____

_____

_____

Where in nature do you most prefer to be and why?

_____

_____

_____

How do you feel when you head out into nature for fresh air and exploring? How is this different from the way you usually feel?

_____

_____

_____

Who do you enjoy sharing outdoor adventures with? What makes them a special addition to this part of your life?

_____

_____

_____

What do you do differently (or similarly) when you are in the great outdoors compared to when you are home or at school?

_____

_____

_____

How do you incorporate singing, whistling, or humming into your daily life? Is it a big or small part of your day?

_____

_____

_____

_____

_____

How does singing, whistling, or humming engage your body and connect you back to yourself?

_____

_____

_____

_____

_____

What would it be like if there were no music, singing, or dancing left in the world? How would that impact you personally?

_____

_____

_____

_____

_____

What does physical affection look like within your family?

_____

_____

_____

When you think of being affectionate with friends and family, what is one way you feel comfortable with physical touch?

_____

_____

_____

Where did you learn how you feel about physical touch? When do you remember first feeling this way about physical touch?

_____

_____

_____

Is there anyone in your life who has a completely different perspective on physical touch? How does this impact your relationship?

_____

_____

_____

_____

Grounding is the process of connecting to the earth. It can reduce stress, improve sleep, and promote feelings of calm. For this practice, all you need is yourself and Mother Nature!

1. Go outside somewhere safe and plant your bare feet on the ground or sit on the earth with as much of your body making contact as possible. (If you have a grass allergy, sit on a blanket with the soles of your feet on the ground.)

2. Take a few deep breaths.

3. Scan your body from head to toe and observe any sensations you may be experiencing.

4. For as long as you like, feel the ground under your body, the warmth of the sun, and the breeze blowing. Hear the animals or trees moving and notice the scents around you.

5. Relax and enjoy!

What do you notice after this practice?
How do you feel physically and/or emotionally?

_____

_____

_____

_____

_____

_____

What's your favorite time of day? What about this time is most meaningful and special to you?

_____

_____

_____

Describe any rituals or special routines you complete during this time:

_____

_____

_____

Do you look forward to this time with nervous excitement or mellow relaxation? How do you feel physically and emotionally when you think about it?

_____

_____

_____

How can you bring those feelings into the rest of your day?

_____

_____

_____

We all have various traits that make us whole. Someone may describe themselves as a motivated, extroverted artist who loves music, cats, and Thai food. What traits describe you?

_____

_____

_____

Describe your best, authentic, and favorite versions of yourself. What are the differences and similarities?

_____

_____

_____

Where do you show up as these different selves?

_____

_____

_____

When and where do you feel most like your true self? What does this look and feel like?

_____

_____

_____

What extracurricular activities do you participate in at school or in your community?

_____

_____

_____

Do your interests inform the activities you sign up for? In what way?

_____

_____

_____

How do your hobbies, sports, and/or extracurriculars engage your senses and activate your body?

_____

_____

_____

What is one new activity you would like to try?

_____

_____

_____

Who makes you feel safe? Who are they to you? What about them brings you a sense of security?

_____

_____

_____

Describe the importance of this person in your life and how your relationship is mutually beneficial:

_____

_____

_____

How does your body know when you are feeling safe or secure?

_____

_____

_____

How do you make others feel safe or secure?

_____

_____

_____

Where do you feel most comfortable? Be specific. For instance, instead of saying, "home," say where exactly. Your room? The den? The kitchen?

_____

_____

_____

What about this place is comforting to you? When you think about it now, what images come to mind and how do you feel in your body?

_____

_____

_____

What people, if any, share this place with you?

_____

_____

Of all the times you have spent in this place, describe your happiest memory:

_____

_____

_____

_____

Visualizing an internal safe or calm place is a helpful technique for when you're feeling emotionally heightened or overwhelmed.

1. Sit comfortably and take a few deep breaths to center yourself.

2. Close your eyes and visualize a place where you feel calm and safe. It can be anywhere you want it to be. It doesn't have to be a place you have ever been or even one that exists in real life.

3. As you visualize this place, notice your surroundings. Where are you? What sounds do you hear? What smells are present? Can you feel or taste anything in this place?

4. Spend as much time here as you would like.

The next time you feel overwhelmed, take a few deep breaths and visualize yourself in this place to help you find calm.

What do you notice after this practice?
How do you feel physically and/or emotionally?

_____

_____

_____

_____

Social media can be both a blessing (think *connection*) and a nightmare (think *pressure and comparison*). Describe the positive and negative attributes of social media:

_____

_____

_____

What are the downsides of growing up in a digital world?

_____

_____

_____

How does social media affect your feelings and your view of yourself and your body?

_____

_____

_____

Where would you like to make changes to your relationship with social media?

_____

_____

_____

How much screen time do you have every day? Is it too much or too little? What do your parents think?

_____

_____

_____

How do you feel when you have a lot of screen time? How about days when you have little?

_____

_____

_____

Describe how you and your parents use technology and social media differently:

_____

_____

_____

What do you think adults don't understand about the way you are growing up versus how they did?

_____

_____

_____

What is your relationship with food?

_____

_____

_____

Think about the concept of fullness and how it pertains to how your body feels. Think about a time you had a delicious meal. How did your body feel physically? How did you feel emotionally?

_____

_____

_____

How do you feel about the concept of certain foods being okay and others unacceptable?

_____

_____

_____

What would you like to see changed in the food, beauty, or diet industries?

_____

_____

_____

Think about the idea of consumption (for instance, food or social media). Describe how it impacts your daily life:

_____

_____

How do you know the difference between someone encouraging you versus pressuring you? What do you notice in your body during these interactions?

_____

_____

_____

What happens when you are feeling pressured by someone and you don't follow your gut instincts?

_____

_____

_____

In what ways might you create a better balance when someone pushes a boundary?

_____

_____

_____

In which areas of your body do you tend to hold tension and tightness?

_____

_____

_____

Describe how your emotions are connected to your physical sensations:

_____

_____

_____

Which do you notice first: physical experiences or emotional feelings?

_____

_____

What is one way you might continue to practice actively noticing physical sensations and connecting them to your feelings to better know yourself?

_____

_____

_____

PART TWO

THINKING ABOUT YOUR THOUGHTS

Some say that the typical person has more than 6,000 thoughts per day, whereas others suggest it can be upward of 50,000! In this section, you will start to notice how your thoughts guide your decisions, practices, beliefs, and emotions. Way back in the day, Descartes, a French philosopher and scientist, said, "I think, therefore I am." But it's also important to understand that thoughts are not feelings, and not all thoughts are true.

This section focuses on your current thought patterns, encourages deeper reflection, and challenges you to identify which thoughts you can work on kicking to the curb. Notice your thoughts and respond to the prompts with honesty and without fear of judgment. The practices will help you focus on impermanence while promoting feelings of centered calmness.

What's on your mind right this very moment?

_____

_____

_____

What is one good thing you are looking forward to today or tomorrow?

_____

_____

_____

What is one thing that hasn't been so great today or yesterday?

_____

_____

_____

How do you generally view the world? Glass half full, half empty, happy to have a glass, or depends on the circumstances? Explain why:

_____

_____

_____

What are your thoughts about school in general?

_____

_____

_____

Think about your classes. Which is your favorite? Which is your least favorite? What about those classes do you like and not like?

_____

_____

_____

When you think about an average school day, what do you look forward to the most?

_____

_____

_____

Which aspects of school create stress for you?

_____

_____

_____

_____

Where do you excel at school? Academics? Sports? Clubs? Student government?

_____

_____

_____

What is your greatest school struggle right now?

_____

_____

What are your family's expectations around grades and participation in clubs and sports? How do they differ from yours, if at all?

_____

_____

_____

Who is your best source of support during school hours? A friend? Teacher? Counselor? Coach? How can they help you overcome your current struggle?

_____

_____

_____

What is your school's policy for phones and social media? Do you agree/disagree with the policy? What would you change?

_____

_____

_____

What is your school's policy on bullying? Do you agree or disagree with the policy? What would you change?

_____

_____

_____

What social media viral challenges have taken place at your school? How does your school manage these challenges?

_____

_____

_____

How do bullying and social media viral challenges influence your ability to stay focused during class?

_____

_____

_____

What are your views on rumors and gossip?

_____

_____

_____

What is a rumor you've heard about yourself? What was this experience like for you?

_____

_____

_____

Describe a time when you stood up for yourself or someone else who was on the receiving end of a rumor or gossip.

_____

_____

_____

How does rumor or gossip influence your relationships?

_____

_____

_____

_____

Our thoughts can run away from us at inconvenient times. This is a useful practice when you need help putting things away so you can focus on what you need to do in that moment.

1. Sit or lie in a comfortable position.

2. Close your eyes. Take a deep breath in for four seconds, hold for five seconds, and release for eight seconds. Do this three times. (This is a 4-5-8 breathing pattern.)

3. Visualize a cubby where you can store your things safely.

4. Remind yourself that the thoughts on your mind are not the most important thing right now, and they will not help you focus or sleep. You can pull them out tomorrow.

5. Visualize yourself picking up all these thoughts and packing them into the cubby for now.

6. Repeat the 4-5-8 breathing pattern in step 2 until you feel calm and relaxed.

What do you notice after this practice?
How do you feel physically and/or emotionally?

_____

_____

_____

_____

_____

_____

What are your goals for the year? To be more social? Join a club? Get a job?

_____

_____

_____

What are your plans after you complete high school?

_____

_____

_____

How do your family's expectations play a role in your goals and plans for after high school? If there were no expectations, would your goals change?

_____

_____

_____

What do you hope your life will look like when you're 25? What will you be doing? Where will you be living?

_____

_____

_____

What is one area of your life where you feel immense pressure to perform?

_____

_____

_____

How often do you find yourself saying, "I should/shouldn't have done this," or, "I should have done better?"

_____

_____

_____

What would be different in your life if you removed the pressure of "should" from yourself and others?

_____

_____

_____

How does "should" help or harm you?

_____

_____

_____

_____

The language of "can/can't" is often limiting. What is something you often say you can or can't do?

_____

_____

_____

Shifting from "can/can't" to "will/won't" helps establish boundaries and encourages decisive action. What is one area of your life where you might shift from "can/can't" to "will/won't"?

_____

_____

_____

What comes up for you when you think about the difference between "can/can't" and "will/won't"?

_____

_____

_____

How will changing from "can/can't" to "will/won't" help or hinder you?

_____

_____

Boundaries create physical and emotional space that allows us to define what we are and are not willing to accept. Where have you seen healthy boundaries modeled for you?

_____

_____

_____

What types of boundaries seem healthy or unhealthy to you?

_____

_____

_____

Where do you struggle with boundaries? Would you like better boundaries in that area?

_____

_____

_____

Where are you really good at establishing boundaries?

_____

_____

_____

_____

Describe a time when a friend or family member set a boundary that encouraged you:

_____

_____

_____

Describe a boundary someone has set that is difficult for you to accept:

_____

_____

_____

How do you honor and respect your boundaries? What about others' boundaries?

_____

_____

_____

What types of boundaries have you found to be helpful?

_____

_____

_____

_____

For this practice, go outside somewhere safe and get comfortable. You will be completing a "nature meditation" and activating your five senses while paying attention to your thoughts.

⭑ Take a few deep breaths to get calm and centered. Your mind may wander during this practice, and that is totally okay.

⭑ Identify five things you can see. Notice the uniqueness of each object or item.

⭑ Notice four things you can feel. Focus on different textures, shapes, sizes, and temperature.

⭑ Listen for three distinct sounds and observe how they are different.

⭑ Identify two things you can smell and notice their unique scents.

⭑ Move your tongue around your mouth or lick your lips. Identify one taste.

What do you notice after this practice?
How do you feel physically and/or emotionally?

_____

_____

_____

_____

_____

How has a lack of boundaries or clear communication led to confusion about your or other people's expectations?

_____

_____

_____

When attempting to meet others' expectations, some people disappoint themselves. Describe a situation when this happened to you:

_____

_____

_____

What matters more to you: disappointing yourself or disappointing others? Explain why:

_____

_____

What would be different in your life if you let go of other people's expectations of you?

_____

_____

_____

What are a few positive aspects of keeping expectations in mind?

_____

_____

_____

Describe which expectations have been helpful and/or motivating for you in the past:

_____

_____

_____

How has working to meet expectations challenged you to overcome an obstacle?

_____

_____

How have you personally encouraged or challenged someone to reach an expectation when they were overwhelmed? What was the outcome?

_____

_____

_____

Make a list of the 10 most important things in your life (it can be anything):

_____

_____

_____

What is the most important thing on your list? Describe why:

_____

_____

_____

What is the least important thing on your list? Describe why:

_____

_____

_____

Where did YOU end up on this list? What do you notice about where you are on the list in comparison to the other things you identified? How can you make yourself more of a priority?

_____

_____

_____

_____

Self-care activities promote health and well-being. What do you do for self-care?

_____

_____

_____

What self-care activities do you enjoy that you learned from your parents or other role models?

_____

_____

_____

What would you like to do for self-care that you are unable to do currently?

_____

_____

_____

What is holding you back from doing those things for yourself? How can you change that?

_____

_____

_____

Describe your current morning and evening routines:

_____

_____

_____

Who has a routine or schedule that you admire? What about it appeals to you?

_____

_____

_____

Do you thrive when your days are calm and structured or when they are random and chaotic? Why do you think this is where you thrive?

_____

_____

_____

What is one change you would like to make in your routine that would provide greater balance and encourage you to prioritize yourself, self-care, and your needs?

_____

_____

"YOUR thoughts have no meaning except the meaning you give them."

—ALFRED ADLER

This visualization practice helps you watch the negative thoughts in your mind float away so that you can feel more at ease.

1. Sit or lie in a comfortable position, close your eyes, and take a few deep breaths.

2. Think of an unpleasant or uncomfortable thought you have been experiencing.

3. Visualize a scene of crashing ocean waves.

4. Scoop up your thoughts and toss them into the waves. Notice how the wave sits for a moment and then moves out of view. Although the thoughts may come back to shore from time to time, the tides take them away. Nothing is permanent, not even these thoughts.

5. Take a few more deep breaths until you feel more at ease.

What do you notice after this practice?
How do you feel physically and/or emotionally?

_____

_____

_____

_____

Do you treat others how you would like to be treated? What are your thoughts around this concept?

_____

_____

_____

If you do not treat others this way, what are your beliefs about people who do? Where did you learn these beliefs?

_____

_____

_____

Does your family influence your beliefs about treating others as you would like to be treated? If so, describe how:

_____

_____

_____

What roles do gratitude and kindness play in this concept?

_____

_____

_____

_____

What is one thing that makes your family unique?

_____

_____

_____

If an outsider were to describe your family, what do you think
would they say?

_____

_____

_____

If your family had a mission statement, what would it be?

_____

_____

_____

What do you think about your family in general? Do you have any
favorite family members? If so, why?

_____

_____

_____

_____

What are the beliefs and values in your family (for example, *Honesty is important, Family is everything,* or *Sundays are for family game night/dinner*)?

_____

_____

_____

Do you share those beliefs and values? Why or why not?

_____

_____

_____

Describe your favorite family tradition and what makes it so important to you:

_____

_____

_____

Where did this tradition begin and why?

_____

_____

_____

Who is your core group of people?

_____

_____

_____

Who are the people you can be truly yourself with, without any filters or fear of judgment?

_____

_____

_____

Who do you turn to for support? Are these the same or different people as the previous two prompts?

_____

_____

_____

How does the support you receive from each of these people differ?

_____

_____

_____

_____

Who are the people you have to wear an emotional mask around or hide parts of yourself from?

_____

_____

_____

What parts of you are you hiding? Why do you hide these parts?

_____

_____

_____

What would be different if you could be yourself around these people?

_____

_____

_____

What is stopping you from being more authentic with them?

_____

_____

_____

This practice consists of doing a full-body scan while paying attention to your thoughts and each body part without judgment.

1. Get comfortable, preferably lying down.

2. Breathe in for four seconds, hold for seven seconds, and release for eight seconds. Repeat this three times. (This is a 4-7-8 breathing pattern.)

3. Notice any physical sensations you may be experiencing.

4. Starting at your feet and working your way up to the top of your head, simply notice each body part and any thoughts that arise. The thoughts could range from gratitude to frustration. Just notice what comes up.

5. As you reach the top of your head, do another round of deep breathing. Acknowledge the thoughts and sensations you have experienced, verbally accept all of them, and thank your body for being your perfect body.

What do you notice after this practice?
How do you feel physically and/or emotionally?

_____

_____

_____

_____

_____

_____

Ghosting is when you completely disappear from someone's life without any notice or warning. When is ghosting appropriate?

_____

_____

_____

Describe a time when you were ghosted and what this experience was like:

_____

_____

_____

Describe a time when you ghosted someone and what this experience was like:

_____

_____

_____

If you could change your experience of being ghosted or ghosting someone else, what would you do differently now?

_____

_____

_____

What are some green flags (signs to move forward) in friendships and relationships?

_____

_____

_____

What are some things you consider red flags (signs to stop)? How might you create boundaries around these?

_____

_____

_____

What are some things that may fall into a yellow flag situation (signs to proceed with caution)? How might you create boundaries around these?

_____

_____

_____

Looking at yourself, what are some things that could be considered red, yellow, or green flags by others?

_____

_____

Identify something that has been troubling you lately, that has been stuck in your mind, and that may be causing worry, stress, or overwhelm:

_____

_____

_____

What are the feelings associated with being stuck?

_____

_____

_____

How will this thing affect you tomorrow, next week, next month, and next year?

_____

_____

_____

How does looking at the larger, longer-term picture affect how you focus on this topic? How does it help alleviate the stress?

_____

_____

_____

What have you learned about money, and who did you learn it from?

_____

_____

_____

What are your beliefs about people who have a lot of money versus those who don't?

_____

_____

_____

What is your relationship with money?

_____

_____

_____

If you won the lottery tomorrow, what would you do with the money and why?

_____

_____

_____

What are your current chores and responsibilities at home?

_____

_____

_____

What are your parents' views on giving you an allowance? Do you agree or disagree?

_____

_____

_____

If your parents stopped taking care of household tasks, what would be different in your life?

_____

_____

_____

How has your family prepared you to live on your own without them? Are you ready? If not, what do you need to focus on?

_____

_____

_____

_____

This practice challenges you to engage the four elements (air, earth, fire, and water) to create a calming atmosphere that helps minimize stress.

1. Air: Take in the deepest breath you can, filling your lungs completely. Hold for a moment, and then release.

2. Earth: Notice whatever part of your body is touching the ground.

3. Fire: Pick a color you associate with fire (red, yellow, orange, white, blue) and locate an object near you that matches.

4. Water: Take a sip of water and notice the sensations you experience from the moment the glass touches your lips to the water reaching your belly.

5. Repeat the first step. As you breathe in, hold, and release, notice what feels the same or different now.

What do you notice after this practice?
How do you feel physically and/or emotionally?

_____

_____

_____

_____

_____

_____

_____

What is your definition of success? How will you know you are successful?

_____

_____

_____

How does this differ from your family's view of success?

_____

_____

_____

What happens if meeting your goal of success disappoints your family?

_____

_____

_____

Can you merge your view of success with your family's view? Why or why not?

_____

_____

_____

What do you think of gratitude and kindness?

_____

_____

_____

When is the most recent time that you were on the receiving end of genuine kindness from someone else?

_____

_____

_____

When was the last time you expressed gratitude and apprecia-tion to someone? What was that experience like for both of you?

_____

_____

_____

Who is the biggest role model for you when it comes to being a kind and gracious person? Describe why:

_____

_____

_____

How do you know you are a valued member of your family? What is your role? How do you participate?

_____

_____

_____

How do you give back to your neighborhood or community? If you had no limitations, where would you like to volunteer and why?

_____

_____

_____

Do you have pleasant or unpleasant associations with the idea of service? Describe your thoughts:

_____

_____

_____

How can you incorporate more giving back to your family, friends, neighborhood, or community?

_____

_____

_____

All bodies are beautiful just the way they are. How do you generally feel about your body?

_____

_____

_____

Our bodies can often be an area where we struggle to love, appreciate, and accept ourselves. In what ways do your thoughts about your body help or harm you?

_____

_____

_____

What purpose does your body serve? Is it cosmetic or practical or both?

_____

_____

_____

What does body positivity mean to you? How would you describe bodily freedom?

_____

_____

_____

How can you use your thoughts in a positive way to encourage body acceptance?

_____

_____

_____

What is one negative thought you have about your own body that you would never think or say about someone else's body?

_____

_____

_____

_____

How can you start to learn to appreciate your body more?

_____

_____

_____

Write one positive affirmation or phrase of encouragement to your body here:

_____

_____

_____

PART THREE

EMOTIONS, EMOTIONS, EMOTIONS

Every single emotion you experience is valid, regardless of what anyone says. You are allowed to and need to feel the full range of emotions available to you; it is part of the human experience. Although all feelings are valid, not all behaviors are healthy or appropriate. It can be hard to move forward in an appropriate way when you haven't processed situations, or if your emotional needs are not met.

Many people try to avoid uncomfortable and unpleasant emotions and seek to only be happy, joyful, or pleasant. In this part, you will be encouraged and challenged to work through the different emotions. It may be helpful to also consider your thoughts about the emotions themselves as well as where they pop up for you physically during the prompts and practices.

What emotions are you most comfortable with and why?

_____

_____

_____

Who has taught you the most about emotional needs and expression? What have you learned?

_____

_____

_____

What more would you like to know about emotions and how to process them?

_____

_____

How would you describe your ability to identify, understand, and express emotions? How would you rate yourself currently on a scale of 1 to 10, where 10 is "super comfortable and satisfied" and 1 is "uncomfortable and unsatisfied"?

_____

_____

_____

What emotions aren't allowed for you personally? Why or
why not?

_____

_____

_____

How do you approach uncomfortable emotions? Are you able to
experience them or do you push them down?

_____

_____

_____

What purpose does avoiding difficult emotions serve you?

_____

_____

_____

What techniques do you notice yourself using to avoid emotions?
How does staying constantly busy or shutting down contribute
to avoidance?

_____

_____

_____

What did you learn from your family (parents, siblings, grandparents, aunts/uncles, cousins) about emotions?

_____

_____

_____

_____

What are the main emotions that are expressed at home? How does each family member express them? (Think of differences between expressing happiness and excitement versus sadness and frustration.)

_____

_____

_____

_____

What emotions aren't allowed in your family? Is this a spoken or an unspoken rule?

_____

_____

_____

_____

_____

How do you know the emotional expectations in different settings? For example, are different emotions and responses allowed in certain places? At home versus school?

_____

_____

_____

What would you like to be different regarding emotional under-standing, acceptance, and expression in your family and why?

_____

_____

_____

How can you encourage that change within your family?

_____

_____

_____

If you could change one thing about how you express emotions personally, what would it be and why? What's stopping you?

_____

_____

_____

Who is the most emotionally expressive person you know?

_____

_____

_____

When you're around that person, how do you feel?

_____

_____

_____

What types of physical expressions (behaviors) are performed in your family (for example, hugging, snuggling, or roughhousing)?

_____

_____

_____

Think about your interactions with your best friend's family. Are the emotional expectations similar to or different from your family's?

_____

_____

_____

_____

Different breathing techniques help you achieve goals and meet specific needs throughout the day. For this practice, you will need a timer and a quiet, comfortable place to sit.

Practice each breathing technique for one minute. Notice the sensations in your body as you move through each of them.

1. **Energize (4-2):** Breathe in for a count of four, release for a count of two.

2. **Balance (4-2-4):** Breathe in for a count of four, hold for a count of two, release for a count of four.

3. **Focus (4-4-4-4):** Breathe in for a count of four, hold for a count of four, release for a count of four, hold for a count of four.

4. **Relax (4-6):** Breathe in for a count of four, release for a count of six.

5. **Restore (5-5-5):** Breathe in for a count of five, hold for a count of five, release for a count of five.

6. **Unwind (4-7-8):** Breathe in for a count of four, hold for a count of seven, release for a count of eight.

What do you notice after this practice?
How do you feel physically and/or emotionally?

_____

_____

_____

_____

How often do you take the time to notice, identify, and name the emotions you experience each day without judgment?

_____

_____

_____

How can you better observe what thoughts come up when you notice a specific emotion?

_____

_____

_____

How often do you notice an uncomfortable emotion and try to push it off? (Spoiler alert: this can prolong the unwanted feeling.)

_____

_____

_____

Describe how you could move toward acknowledging, accepting, releasing, and moving forward when emotions arise:

_____

_____

_____

How do emotions make you weak or strong? Does sharing your emotions make you weak or strong?

_____

_____

_____

Where did you learn these beliefs?

_____

_____

_____

How would you like to shift your thoughts so that you can be more emotionally expressive?

_____

_____

_____

What emotions specifically would you like to learn to be more comfortable with?

_____

_____

_____

_____

How do you suppress or exaggerate emotions?

_____

_____

_____

Which people make you feel the most comfortable when
expressing your emotions?

_____

_____

_____

Who in your life makes it feel uncomfortable to be emotionally
expressive?

_____

_____

_____

What would be different if you could voice your emotional needs
without fear of judgment? Are your fears valid? Why or why not?

_____

_____

_____

_____

Do you tend to live your life from an emotional or a rational/
logical stance?

_____

_____

_____

How would you describe your parents' styles? Are they rational/
logical, emotional, neither, or both?

_____

_____

_____

How does rational/logical thinking help guide your
decision-making processes?

_____

_____

_____

What can you do to incorporate emotions with logical/rational
thinking when making daily choices?

_____

_____

_____

"Love" is defined as "constant affection for a person." I believe that "love" is a verb that requires continued intentional commitment to and acceptance of the other person. How do you define "love"?

_____

_____

_____

How do you know you are loved in general? How do you know your family and friends love you?

_____

_____

_____

What do you do to show those you care about that you love them?

_____

_____

_____

How do you show yourself love?

_____

_____

_____

Next time you're experiencing a strong emotion, try this exercise. Although simple, this is an immensely powerful activity to help you accept the full range of emotions you experience, especially when you are feeling overwhelmed, stressed, or anxious.

1. Sit in a comfortable position and choose one breathing exercise from page 79. Breathe for at least two minutes.

2. Identify the emotion you are experiencing: _____

3. Choose one: *I notice this feeling as being temporarily a) pleasant or b) unpleasant.*

4. Notice where you feel this emotion in your body: _____

5. Say the following out loud:

   - *It is okay for me to feel (state the emotion).*

   - *I am allowed to feel (state the emotion).*

   - *I need to feel (state the emotion).*

   - *I give myself permission to feel (state the emotion).*

6. Identify what you need to accept and cope with this emotion: _____

7. Take three deep healing breaths and release everything.

What do you notice after this practice?
How do you feel physically and/or emotionally?

_____

_____

_____

Happiness can be described as feeling pleasure, well-being, contentment, and/or enjoyment. Where do you feel happiest and why?

_____

_____

_____

How do you know when you are happy?

_____

_____

_____

What most recently made you happy and brought a smile to your face?

_____

_____

_____

Who are you the happiest around? What is it about this person that encourages this feeling?

_____

_____

_____

Joy is a feeling of prolonged, great happiness. When was the last time you felt truly joyful? What were you doing? Who was there?

_____

_____

_____

How do you incorporate small moments of joy into your day?

_____

_____

_____

What is a small act of kindness you could do today to bring joy to someone else?

_____

_____

_____

If you were the president, what rule or law would you establish to guarantee a moment of joy in everyone's day?

_____

_____

_____

_____

How do you feel about surprises? Do you love or loathe them? Why?

_____

_____

_____

When was the last time you felt surprised or someone was able to pull off a surprise for you?

_____

_____

_____

What would be a good surprise that could happen to you today?

_____

_____

_____

What emotions do you associate with being surprised?

_____

_____

_____

_____

Excitement is a heightened state of eagerness, enthusiasm, and energy. What is something you are excited about or looking forward to?

_____

_____

_____

How do you behave when you are excited? How is this similar to or different from when you are not excited?

_____

_____

_____

Who in your life do you get most excited about spending time with? Why?

_____

_____

What in your life makes you consistently excited? How can you bring that feeling into other aspects of your life?

_____

_____

_____

The dictionary describes "bravery" as feeling mentally or morally strong, or showing no fear. How would you describe being brave or courageous?

_____

_____

_____

Sometimes being brave means acknowledging when you're scared and not doing something you're uncomfortable with. When was the last time you were brave in this way?

_____

_____

_____

Describe the bravest thing you have ever done:

_____

_____

_____

Who is the bravest or most courageous person you know? What is inspiring about them and their story?

_____

_____

_____

This practice uses your breath and matches it with the rhythm of your heartbeat to help reduce stress and promote peace and gratitude.

1. Sit comfortably and shake off negative vibes to start shifting into a place of positivity and gratitude.

2. Focus on the part of your chest where your heart is located.

3. Place your hand on your heart. Breathe normally, but visualize your breath coming directly from your heart.

4. Continue breathing from and through your heart with positivity and gratitude for your life. Notice the positive physical sensations you are feeling.

5. Focus on feeling calm, relaxed, present, and peaceful. Keep breathing.

6. Give this practice a name. Use this name as a mental cue to match your breath to your heartbeat whenever you feel overwhelmed or like you need a shift in attitude.

What do you notice after this practice?
How do you feel physically and/or emotionally?

_____

_____

_____

_____

_____

_____

What is the most confusing part of your life right now? How do conflicting messages you receive contribute to this confusion?

_____

_____

_____

Does feeling confused make you feel frustrated, overwhelmed, curious, excited, or a combination of things? Explain why:

_____

_____

_____

When you're confused, what cues do you receive from your body?

_____

_____

_____

Boundaries help create clarity and minimize confusion. What is an area in your life where you could decrease confusion by implementing a boundary?

_____

_____

_____

When in your life have you experienced sadness or grief (deep, profound sadness or suffering)?

_____

_____

_____

How were you comforted or supported during this time? Who, if anyone, comforted you?

_____

_____

_____

Describe a time when you supported or comforted someone who was sad or grieving:

_____

_____

_____

What is something you wish others knew about your experiences with sadness and grief?

_____

_____

_____

What is currently the biggest source of frustration in your life?

_____

_____

_____

How do you feel physically and emotionally when you are
presented with this obstacle?

_____

_____

_____

In what way do you currently manage your frustration? How
does this help or harm you?

_____

_____

_____

How can you be more accepting of the experiences that
contribute to feelings of frustration?

_____

_____

_____

_____

How do you express anger? How does it feel in your body?

_____

_____

_____

Describe a time when your anger overwhelmed you and
you reacted in a way that wasn't in alignment with your
emotional needs:

_____

_____

_____

How would you like to respond to, process, and cope with
situations or people who invoke anger in you in the future?

_____

_____

_____

What other uncomfortable emotions does anger cover up for you
(for instance, sadness, disappointment, or feeling unimportant or
disrespected)?

_____

_____

_____

How could confronting your biggest fear change your life? What would be different for you?

_____

_____

_____

When you experience a situation where you feel scared, do you recognize the physical sensation or emotion first? Describe how these emotions manifest for you:

_____

_____

_____

Which people know your biggest fears? Why did you choose to share this vulnerable piece of yourself with them?

_____

_____

_____

Describe a time when you had to do something that made you scared:

_____

_____

_____

This practice creates a long-term storage solution for past experiences that may be contributing to distress.

1. Visualize a container that can hold all the hard things you are having trouble carrying in your life right now. The container can be anything from an industrial safe to a massive amethyst geode with a latch and lid.

2. Put all the things you are carrying into this container (for example, a breakup, overwhelming responsibilities, or an old argument).

3. When the container is full, place the lid on, and make sure it is secure.

4. Put it away where it will be safe. You aren't throwing it away or donating it; it's just being stored until you have the resources to unpack, sort through, and handle it.

5. Take a deep breath, acknowledge its importance, and walk away.

What do you notice after this practice?
How do you feel physically and/or emotionally?

_____

_____

_____

_____

_____

_____

Describe a situation that was embarrassing at the time, but now you look back on and laugh:

_____

_____

_____

Describe a situation that was embarrassing and still makes you uncomfortable:

_____

_____

_____

What are the similarities and differences between these two stories?

_____

_____

_____

What is the worst thing your family has ever done that embarrassed you? From their perspective and assuming positive intent, what may they have been trying to accomplish?

_____

_____

_____

What is a food you can't stand? How do you respond physically and emotionally when presented with this item?

_____

_____

_____

What is something that is socially acceptable, but you have a great aversion to?

_____

_____

_____

Name something or someone you loathe and explain why:

_____

_____

_____

What would be different if you were able to look at things from the perspective of that individual or situation? How would your view of loathing or disgust change?

_____

_____

_____

Contempt is a feeling of disdain, lack of respect, or the act of despising. Describe a time when you felt disrespected by someone and it led to contempt:

_____

_____

_____

What is a deal-breaker for you in any relationship (for example, dishonesty, stealing, or disrespect)? Why?

_____

_____

_____

How might a lack of respect for others cause them distress?

_____

_____

_____

How do you handle a situation or person you do not respect or feel is unworthy of your attention or affection?

_____

_____

_____

Describe a time when you felt hurt by someone else and kept it to yourself:

_____

_____

_____

When you think of this experience, what comes up for you now, physically and emotionally?

_____

_____

_____

How could it be beneficial for you to discuss your hurt with that person?

_____

_____

_____

How do you receive comfort from yourself or others when you experience hurt? How can you advocate for yourself to have increased support during times like this in the future?

_____

_____

_____

Where in your life do you lack self-confidence and tend to feel insecure?

_____

_____

_____

Who knows you might struggle in this area? Is it obvious or hidden? How does this affect your daily life?

_____

_____

_____

Who else do you know who has a similar challenge? How might you support one another?

_____

_____

_____

How do you want to feel when you face this insecurity in the future? What can you do to slowly build more self-confidence in this area?

_____

_____

_____

This practice incorporates music and movement. You will need your phone, a stereo, or record player. (I'd personally pick vinyl over digital if I had the option!)

1. Think of your favorite song in the whole world, why it's your favorite, and the emotions you associate with it. Notice how you respond just thinking about it.

2. Turn on the song as loud as you feel comfortable and allow yourself to move with the music. Remember—no one is watching, so just feel through the experience.

3. Notice how your body moves and sways to the rhythm, any physical sensations you experience, and how this song makes you feel.

4. Repeat if necessary and time permits!

What do you notice after this practice?
How do you feel physically and/or emotionally?

_____

_____

_____

_____

_____

_____

_____

_____

What would happen if you shifted from fear of missing out (FOMO) to joy of missing out (JOMO)—not waiting for the next best thing to bring you happiness?

_____

_____

_____

How does social media influence your ability to be content with yourself?

_____

_____

_____

In what ways are you content with your life in the present moment?

_____

_____

_____

Who is the most content and satisfied person you know? What are the differences and similarities in how you approach life?

_____

_____

_____

How do you know when you are satisfied—emotionally, physically, spiritually, and mentally?

_____

_____

_____

What would others observe about you to let them know you were having a good time?

_____

_____

_____

How does seeking a good time or pleasure cause distress in other areas of your life?

_____

_____

What is one area of your life that is simply not a good time? Where could you make a shift and find appreciation for your circumstances in those times?

_____

_____

_____

Peace is a state of being untroubled, quiet, and tranquil. What does it feel like when your body and mind are peaceful?

_____

_____

_____

Where in your life could you scale back on activities, people, and/ or expectations to encourage greater feelings of peacefulness?

_____

_____

_____

In what ways are you scared or apprehensive about making these changes?

_____

_____

_____

What is one small step you could take for yourself today to begin working toward a more balanced environment?

_____

_____

_____

Pride is happiness through accomplishment, or a feeling of importance. What are you most proud of in your life right now?

_____

_____

_____

Describe the process of what it took to reach that accomplishment, including what emotions come up for you and any physical sensations you notice:

_____

_____

_____

If you asked your family why they are most proud of you, what would they say?

_____

_____

_____

How do you know when others are proud of you?

_____

_____

_____

Gratitude is a feeling of contentment, satisfaction, and appreciation. List five things for which you are grateful:

_____

_____

_____

Pick one thing from your list and describe how it impacts your life:

_____

_____

_____

List five people in your life whom you appreciate:

_____

_____

_____

Think about how you like to be shown appreciation and gratitude. What can you do to show the people on your list that you are grateful for them?

_____

_____

_____

_____

PART FOUR

CHALLENGE & CHANGE BEHAVIORS

Change can be both exciting and overwhelming! Many people struggle with the uncertainty of the unknown on the other side of change. It takes courage to be vulnerable and to identify where you may want or need to make a shift. Change can be very uncomfortable at times, and that's okay—you need to get out of your comfort zone, leave the familiar behind, and embrace the promise of change!

A couple of my favorite quotes about change include, "If you don't like something, change it. If you can't change it, change your attitude," and, "If nothing changes, then nothing changes." They are both powerful reminders that you can create change, whether it is your circumstances or your viewpoint. In this section, you will be challenged to identify changes you may want to make and create an action plan to begin making those shifts, drawing on the first three parts of the book.

What do you think is needed for someone to change in general?

_____

_____

_____

How do you think change occurs? What needs to be present?

_____

_____

_____

Why do you think some people struggle with challenging their thoughts and creating change?

_____

_____

_____

Who is one person in your life that is really good at change? What do you admire about their attitude? What qualities do you share with this person?

_____

_____

_____

When you think of change, are you excited, nervous, or both?

_____

_____

_____

Describe which aspects of change are exciting to you and which parts feel overwhelming or cause nervousness:

_____

_____

_____

What is one area of your life where you are excited to make change?

_____

_____

_____

Where are you hesitant or stressed out about creating change?

_____

_____

_____

_____

In what areas of your life do you most struggle with embracing change?

_____

_____

_____

Where do you feel most comfortable going with the ebbs and flows, or the unknown aspects, of change?

_____

_____

_____

Describe a time when you once thought something about an idea but changed your opinion:

_____

_____

_____

Describe a time when you changed your mind about a person (for better or worse):

_____

_____

_____

What is one behavior or action you don't love that you would like to stop doing? Where did you learn this behavior?

_____

_____

_____

What is holding you back from stopping this behavior or action?

_____

_____

_____

How will making this change influence your life?

_____

_____

_____

What is one small step you could take today to begin stopping that behavior or action?

_____

_____

_____

_____

What behaviors do you have that are helpful? How do you know they are helpful?

_____

_____

_____

Describe a time when you reacted to a situation and someone complimented your behavior:

_____

_____

_____

With regard to how you think, feel, or act, what is one thing about which you are really proud of yourself?

_____

_____

_____

Where did you learn this type of behavior?

_____

_____

_____

This practice consists of a full-body scan while paying attention to the physical sensations you experience in each body part, without judgment.

1. Get comfortable, either in a seated position or lying down.

2. Breathe in for a count of four, hold for a count of seven, and release for a count of eight. Repeat a few times. (This is a 4-7-8 breathing pattern.)

3. Notice how you feel overall. Do you feel any tension or tightness, or areas that are relaxed, calm, or neutral?

4. Starting at the top of your head and working your way down to your feet, breathe deeply and pause at each part of your body. Notice the physical sensations.

5. As you reach your feet, do another round of deep breathing. Slowly scan back up to the top of your head and notice if the sensations have shifted.

What do you notice after this practice?
How do you feel physically and/or emotionally?

_____

_____

_____

_____

_____

_____

_____

Which of your behaviors or reactions are unhelpful? How may they be harmful to you?

_____

_____

_____

How do you know they are unhelpful or harmful?

_____

_____

_____

Describe a time when you had a potentially harmful emotional reaction or engaged in an unhelpful behavior and what happened as a result:

_____

_____

_____

How would you like to handle this type of situation in the future?

_____

_____

_____

_____

Overgeneralizing is when an issue is blown out of proportion to the extreme. It often sounds like "always," "never," "everybody," and "nobody." Where in your life do you tend to overgeneralize?

_____

_____

_____

What emotions are you usually experiencing when you notice yourself overgeneralizing?

_____

_____

_____

How does overgeneralizing help or harm you and your relationships?

_____

_____

_____

Describe how you might begin to shift out of overgeneralizing in conversations and/or interactions with others:

_____

_____

_____

All-or-nothing thinking (aka black-and-white or polarized thinking) leads people to think in extremes; things are either good or bad, right or wrong, a success or a failure. Where do you struggle with all-or-nothing thinking?

_____

_____

_____

How do you feel physically and emotionally after responding to the above prompt?

_____

_____

_____

What fact-based statement counteracts your initial response?

_____

_____

_____

Write a true statement that promotes supporting yourself and positive growth that falls somewhere in the gray area:

_____

_____

_____

Catastrophizing is when you think of the worst possible scenario or outcome, causing yourself undue anxiety and stress. Describe your experience with catastrophizing:

_____

_____

_____

How would you support someone who tends to think the worst-case scenario will happen?

_____

_____

_____

When do you find yourself most likely to catastrophize?

_____

_____

_____

What would you like to do differently in similar situations in the future?

_____

_____

_____

Filtering is when we focus only on the negative, discounting the positive (for example, calling yourself a bad student for getting a C when you expected an A). Describe a time when you did this:

_____

_____

_____

What truth challenges those negative thoughts?

_____

_____

_____

What would be different if you could stop filtering as soon as you recognize it happening?

_____

_____

_____

When you notice you are filtering, what can you do to challenge your thoughts?

_____

_____

_____

This practice is a random object mindfulness practice. Wherever you are, notice the closest object or item to your left or right; it can be anything that isn't an electronic device.

1. Set a timer for five minutes and begin to observe the selected object.

2. Think of the purpose or importance of the object.

3. Pick up the object if possible, hold it in your hand(s), and simply sit with it.

4. Notice the colors, patterns, textures, temperature, and shape of this item. If it has a smell or taste, notice this as well.

5. When the timer goes off, notice if your view of the object's purpose or importance has changed.

What do you notice after this practice?
How do you feel physically and/or emotionally?

_____

_____

_____

_____

_____

_____

_____

_____

Labeling is when we focus on negative aspects of ourselves that aren't true (for example, "My friend didn't text me back; they think I'm a loser.") Describe a time when you did this:

_____

_____

_____

What positive statement could replace that negative label?

_____

_____

_____

How have you labeled someone else? What might help you better understand their perspective without using a negative label?

_____

_____

_____

What will you do to limit unnecessary labeling of yourself or others?

_____

_____

_____

Fortune-telling is when we believe we know what will happen (usually negative), make assumptions about a person or situation, and may jump to conclusions. Describe a time when you did this:

_____

_____

_____

Was there a time that your "crystal ball" was wrong, and you made an assumption that you learned was incorrect?

_____

_____

When you go into fortune-telling mode, are you trying to protect yourself or others?

_____

_____

_____

How can you avoid fortune-telling in the future?

_____

_____

_____

Mind reading is when we believe we know what others are thinking (or will think) about us; it generally isn't positive or pleasant. How is mind reading helpful or harmful?

_____

_____

_____

Describe a time when you were on the receiving end of someone else's mind reading:

_____

_____

_____

What questions could you ask yourself and others to avoid falling into the mind-reading trap?

_____

_____

How will your friendships and other relationships improve when mind reading is removed?

_____

_____

_____

When you're dealing with the cognitive distortions discussed in the previous pages, it can be difficult to assume that other people have positive intentions. What people or circumstances make you feel apprehensive or defensive?

_____

_____

_____

What would be different if you assumed positive intent or that the person was doing their best?

_____

_____

Who do you want to have a changed or different relationship with?

_____

_____

_____

How might you make a shift to change and grow in this relationship?

_____

_____

_____

You are halfway through the last section of this book! Think about what has already shifted for you. What has been the most surprising thing you have learned about yourself up until now?

_____

_____

What has been difficult or frustrating for you to work through so far?

_____

_____

_____

Where do you believe you have the most room for growth right now?

_____

_____

What are you most looking forward to in your journey of self-discovery?

_____

_____

_____

Our vagus nerve spans from the brain to the abdomen. It is the main part of our "rest and digest" system (the parasympathetic nervous system). Stimulating this nerve through activities like singing and humming can help improve mood, minimize anxiety, and reduce stress. This practice will help stimulate your vagus nerve.

1. In a standing position, take a deep breath in. As you exhale, make the *om* or *vu* sound. Continue humming this sound with each out breath.

2. Next, raise your shoulders up to your ears and forcefully drop them down.

3. Notice your pelvis and hips, and do any movement that feels good and reduces tension (for instance, moving back and forth or in a hula-hoop motion).

4. Finally, alternately tap your toes and heels.

5. Repeat the sequence for a few minutes. Notice how stimulating your vagus nerve feels to you.

What do you notice after this practice?
How do you feel physically and/or emotionally?

_____

_____

_____

_____

_____

_____

Where do you feel the most balanced and self-confident at school?

_____

_____

_____

Where do you struggle the most in school?

_____

_____

_____

What types of external and internal pressure contribute to the area you struggle with?

_____

_____

_____

Where can you establish a realistic boundary to help minimize your struggles? How will this boundary encourage positive growth for you academically?

_____

_____

_____

Have your parents ever set a rule or expectation that doesn't make sense to you? What can you ask them for a better understanding to minimize your frustration or confusion?

_____

_____

_____

How would discussing boundaries with your family improve your relationships and life in general?

_____

_____

_____

What are you most worried about when discussing boundaries with your family?

_____

_____

_____

How would you like to respond if a boundary is violated?

_____

_____

_____

Describe a time when you said yes to a friend or social event when that meant saying no to yourself and how you felt about it:

_____

_____

_____

How can setting boundaries in friendships support you having your needs met?

_____

_____

_____

What stops you from setting boundaries with your friends?

_____

_____

_____

How might you show kindness to your friends while you establish and maintain a boundary you know you will benefit from setting?

_____

_____

_____

_____

Describe your relationship with your phone and social media:

_____

_____

_____

What would it be like to live in a home with only one phone for the whole family that is also the only way to get online?

_____

_____

_____

If you could shift your approach to using your phone, would you? Why or why not?

_____

_____

_____

How old were you when you received your first phone? If you could go back, would you encourage your parents to change their minds? Why or why not?

_____

_____

_____

What is one thing you would love to be able to say yes to right now?

_____

_____

_____

What is one area of your life where it would be really freeing to step back, quit, or say no?

_____

_____

_____

How is your ability to say yes, no, or slow down and/or stop something influenced by your concern about other people's expectations?

_____

_____

_____

How can you make one small step forward in saying no to something that isn't serving you?

_____

_____

_____

Bilateral stimulation is a rhythmic movement that occurs in a left-to-right pattern. It helps your nervous system orient to new stimuli while decreasing worry. This can be achieved through visual (following a light), auditory (a repetitive beat that toggles from left to right ear), or tactile (tapping or buzzing sensation) stimuli. This practice focuses on tactile stimuli.

1. Begin in a comfortable position. Cross your arms over your chest with the tips of your fingers resting on your shoulders or collarbone. You can also rest your hands on your knees or next to your legs.

2. Breathe at a slow and steady pace, and slowly begin tapping (count one, pause, count two, pause, repeat), alternating from left to right.

3. Continue tapping and breathing for at least five minutes.

What do you notice after this practice?
How do you feel physically and/or emotionally?

_____

_____

_____

_____

_____

_____

_____

Are you a planner, a worrier, or both? How much time on average do you spend planning and worrying?

_____

_____

_____

In what ways does planning or making lists help minimize your feelings of stress and overwhelm?

_____

_____

_____

Does worrying benefit your ability to live your life to the fullest? Why or why not?

_____

_____

_____

Where can you release unnecessary worry? What will you do with the extra time you have not spent focused on worrying?

_____

_____

_____

Describe the last time you were critical with yourself:

_____

_____

_____

What would you tell a friend who had a similar experience? How is this different from how you speak to yourself?

_____

_____

_____

What is one negative thought you tend to have about yourself?

_____

_____

_____

Write one positive thought you can think about yourself instead of that negative thought and repeat it to yourself daily:

_____

_____

_____

_____

Are you a morning person or a night owl? Describe why you have this preference:

_____

_____

_____

How do you typically approach mornings? What is your current morning routine?

_____

_____

_____

In what ways do you focus on yourself after school? What is your current evening routine?

_____

_____

_____

What can you do to make yourself a priority for at least 10 minutes every morning and every evening?

_____

_____

_____

How frequently does your daily schedule allow for "me time" or space to just rest?

_____

_____

_____

What does rest mean to you? In what ways do you rest, relax, and recharge?

_____

_____

_____

If you could remove one thing from your schedule, what would it be and why?

_____

_____

_____

What are you afraid will happen if you remove this one thing to allow more space for yourself?

_____

_____

_____

If time and money were of no concern, what would you start right now?

_____

_____

_____

If you could gift everyone in your life one thing, what would it be and why?

_____

_____

_____

How are your future goals reflected in what you would start and what you would give?

_____

_____

_____

What feeling do you hope to achieve in starting this thing and giving this specific gift? What is something small you could do now to accomplish the same feeling?

_____

_____

_____

When we grab our phones, we often fall into a mindless loop of scrolling that can lead to comparison, judgment, self-criticism, and hours of time lost. For this practice, grab your phone or computer and head to your favorite social app.

1. Before you start, set an intention to understand and validate why you're going on social media. For example, "I am searching for wardrobe inspiration, and I am happy with my current clothing options."

2. Notice what emotions you're feeling and how your body responds.

3. Allow yourself to approach this time without judgment.

4. As you scroll, identify one thing for which you are grateful or appreciate coming across.

5. Notice what you learn. Ask how this information benefits you and how it may spark joy and happiness. If it doesn't make you feel great, consider the possibility of unfollowing the account.

What do you notice after this practice?
How do you feel physically and/or emotionally?

_____

_____

_____

_____

_____

What are you afraid to start because you are worried it won't be perfect?

_____

_____

_____

In what areas of your life do you strive for perfection? Do you expect others to meet the same standards? Why or why not?

_____

_____

_____

How would your life be better if you let go of perfectionistic tendencies?

_____

_____

_____

What can you do to release the pressure to meet any unrealistic standards you have set for yourself?

_____

_____

_____

If you weren't worried about the opinions of others, what would you want to do with your life?

_____

_____

_____

When do you trust yourself the most?

_____

_____

_____

What would it be like to trust yourself consistently without hesitation or judgment?

_____

_____

_____

What is one small thing you can start today to begin working toward feeling more confident in your decisions?

_____

_____

_____

_____

When you are having a rough day, what is your go-to process to get out of a funky mood?

_____

_____

_____

What is your favorite form of self-care?

_____

_____

_____

What do you enjoy about the weekend? What do you most look forward to?

_____

_____

_____

Look at your first three answers on this page. How can you incorporate them into your daily life to lift your mood more consistently?

_____

_____

_____

What are your favorite and least favorite qualities or characteristics in your parents?

_____

_____

_____

How are you similar to or different from your parents?

_____

_____

_____

What have learned from your parents that you value most?

_____

_____

_____

Where can you find gratitude and appreciation in both your favorite and least favorite qualities in yourself and your parents?

_____

_____

_____

_____

What consistently brings you joy?

_____

_____

_____

What does your dream day look like? Think of how you would wake up and what you would do all the way until you hop back into bed at night. Who would be there? What would you do?

_____

_____

_____

_____

Describe a kindness you recently received:

_____

_____

What are three things you can start doing today to get you closer to having your dream day, every day?

_____

_____

_____

_____

resources

This section leads with a list of helplines that can offer immediate, specific support. For longer-term help, talk to a trusted adult such as a parent, teacher, or doctor to determine the next steps in finding a therapist. Several directories are included here to help you begin the search; ask your caregiver to check with your insurance to determine coverage.

TELEPHONE SUPPORT

Caregiver Help Desk: 855-227-3640
Crisis Text Line: Text HOME to 741741
Disaster Distress Helpline: 800-985-5990
Domestic Violence Hotline: 800-799-SAFE (7233) / text LOVEIS to 22522
National Alliance on Mental Illness HelpLine: 800-950-NAMI (6264)
Substance Abuse & Mental Health Services Administration National
    Helpline: 800-662-HELP (4357)
Partnership for Drug-Free America Helpline: 855-378-4373
Sexual Assault Hotline: 800-656-HOPE (4673)
StrongHearts Native Helpline: 844-762-8483 (for Native Americans and
    Alaska Natives)
Suicide Prevention Lifeline: 800-273-TALK (8255)
Trans Lifeline: 877-565-8860 (trans peer support)
The Trevor Project: 866-488-7386 / text START to 678678 (suicide
    prevention)

THERAPIST DIRECTORIES

Good Therapy: GoodTherapy.org
Inclusive Therapists: InclusiveTherapists.com
Open Path Psychotherapy Collective (reduced-rate and sliding-scale services
    for under- and uninsured individuals): OpenPathCollective.com
Psychology Today: PsychologyToday.com
Therapy Den: TherapyDen.com

references

Breit, S., A. Kupferberg, G. Rogler, and G. Hasler. "Vagus Nerve as Modulator of the Brain-Gut Axis in Psychiatric and Inflammatory Disorders." *Frontiers in Psychiatry* (2018). DOI.org/10.3389/fpsyt.2018.00044.

Guy-Evans, O. (May 18, 2021). "Parasympathetic Nervous System Functions." Simply Psychology. SimplyPsychology.org/parasympathetic-nervous -system.html.

Kabat-Zinn, Jon. *Wherever You Go, There You Are: Mindfulness in Everyday Life (10th Edition)*. New York: Hyperion, 1994.

McCallie, M. S., C. M. Blum, and C. J. Hood. "Progressive Muscle Relaxation." *Journal of Human Behavior in the Social Environment* 13, no. 3 (2008): 51-66.

Nelson, J. B. "Mindful Eating: The Art of Presence While You Eat." *Diabetes Spectrum* 30, no. 3 (2017): 171-174. DOI.org/10.2337/ds17-0015.

Parnell, Laurel. *Tapping In: A Step-by-Step Guide to Activating Your Healing Resources through Bilateral Stimulation: Reduce Anxiety, Sleep Better, Overcome Trauma.* Boulder, CO: Sounds True, 2008.

Shapiro, Francine. *Eye Movement Desensitization and Reprocessing: Basic Principles, Protocols, and Procedures (2nd Edition)*. New York: Guilford Press, 2001.

Tawwab, Nedra Glover. *Set Boundaries, Find Peace: A Guide to Reclaiming Yourself*. New York: TarcherPerigee, 2021.

ABOUT the AUTHOR

Kristina Dingus Keuhlen, PhD, LMFT, is a licensed marriage and family therapist and founder of North Texas Family Therapy, PLLC. She specializes in anxiety disorders, grief, and trauma, using cognitive behavioral therapy and eye movement desensitization and reprocessing therapy through a mindfulness lens.

In her private practice, she provides psychotherapy to individuals who struggle with overachieving and perfectionism as well as parent-teen relationship dynamics to help her clients live lives that are aligned with their most authentic selves and deepest desires. Find more information and additional resources at NorthTexasFamilyTherapy.com.